HARD DECISIONS EASY LIFE

DEEPAK GUPTA

Contents

More From 30 Minutes Read Series

Book 1: How to Heal Yourself
    Book 2: Alone than Lonely
    Book 3: Happiness without Cause
    Book 4: Being Busy is not always Productive
    Book 5: How to Deal with Haters
    Book 6: Hard Decisions Easy Life
    Book 7: Sell Your Talent

The Beginning Of Your Decisions: You Took A Decision

First of all, I want to say 'Thank You'and respect your decision to spend your hard-earned money on a small book. I hope I will keep the trust intact as you were entered with it. *You decided to buy this book but I believe it doesn't matter how many you spend but how well you utilize your money in the right place.*It's not about quantity but the quality. A simple talk, success doesn't come with money but with smart decisions. A quick mover advantage can be the part of your decision but how well you innovate and make unique decisions can also handle your late future decisions. **If you make unique decisions, you don't need to wait in the queue because you will always be the first in your innovation and that's why unique artists sell more than anyone.**It's not about more but about a unique style of taking the decisions. You took a decision to spend your money on my book but until you understand it well; your money remains the money. Best decisions convert art and money into values.

Hard decisions and Easy Life seems good in the 21st century or it should be named as Smart Decisions and Easy Life. Okay as we are living in the digital generation, people tell us to make smart decisions. Someday I also told you the same but we need to be smart and hard on our decisions in which hard decisions are for understanding the Bandersnatch of life. Once I watched a movie **Black Mirror: Bandersnatch**and I understand one principle of success. It told us to keep repeating the self valued decisions until we make it right. *Every question has many answers but how well and smartly we understand and achieve it, make us a better decision-maker.*

When you take any decision and it gets wrong, don't quit but make some modifications to your current goal. Be dynamic like **Charles Darwin**said. The most responsive to the environment can take the right decisions. *When you get bored with everyday food, you don't stop eating the food but replacing it with good delicious food.*Just like when you feel you are taking wrong decisions, insert some improvements, and take it again. More dynamic responsiveness can result in better decision making.

Hard decisions make our minds more responsive and give us better direction to become better leaders. In the stock market, if you have the patience to bear the loss then you can take tough decisions and one day you will win. It's like to keep stand firm instead of running back. Some decisions in life are pre-decided like we spend a huge amount of money on entertainment because it's the part of our recreation. We don't compromise with family emotions and comfort. We purchase products online and go with offers. These are daily lifestyle decisions but affect us in the long term. Let's understand a new term in decision making. Whatever you read, please implement it too. *There's no use of reading until we apply and learn. That's a great decision too.*

CHAPTER ONE

THE LONG CHAIN OF DECISIONS IN BANDERSNATCH

As an author, I can assure you, you learn by applying not by understanding. We plan everything as a family or an individual but once you plan with the point of view of the world, you can crack any riddle easily. *According to the world, if you take decision with the point of view of a large audience, you would get close to the best decision-maker.*Understand the marketers, how well they understand customer's tumult, and provide them the products and services they don't even know. Our output and success depend on a series of decisions. Nothing gets to grow in a day and nothing can ruin in a day. Your medical bills are positively correlated with your eating, sleeping, and meditation habits. If you do anything wrong, you have to face it one day. Your current position is the cumulative decisions of your life. Your old decisions decide your life journey.

If we allow or teach a child to bully someone in his school then it may become his behaviour and habits. How well we teach ourselves to take better decisions, the better we will be. In my opinion, every decision we take has two or more options whether the decision is right or wrong. Irrespective of its right or wrong quality, the decision opens a new world of web and it has options too. ***No decision is right or wrong. We make it wrong or right with how well we perceive it in our minds.***Suppose you love to sing but for some reason, you become an engineer then you will also have the chance to get success when you take and accept it in your mind. Our right or wrong in any decision depends on how well we walk on the web. Many people got succeed in different areas because they accepted their decision. Believe in your decisions can make it right or wrong. You can take wrong decisions but still be succeeded. As I said, every time you take a decision, it opens a new web of new decisions. Understand the options of your life to learn the real sense of decision making.

The conclusion of any decision depends on how well we accept and work on it. You can make wrong decisions but can make it right with your will.

CHAPTER TWO

The World of Possibilities

We can also take hard decisions to do the work with our will than to look for someone who can do it for us. It can happen due to lack of money, trust, or believe in ourselves to do the work better.

There's always a world of possibilities when it comes to take hard decisions and trust me this will help you to learn, understand, and save your money. Your one decision affect the other and the other affects another and this series never stopped just like criminals and liars keep repeating their mistakes. We all are not a drawing master but we still draw pictures when we were in kindergarten because we have a series of decisions at a very early age. Some become the great painters too. We need to learn this with the help of a good instance and I think my life has better to offer you. For the authors, the biggest problem starts after writing. We need a publisher to publish our books and a huge amount of money with very little chance of getting succeeded but this decision can be better if we learn and do everything by ourselves. That's our first decision and now our next decisions will be based on our primary decisions.

I have learned to publish and understand the art of offering real value to readers. When you take such hard decisions, you learn better than to offer your work to someone else. I design my covers, formatting my ebook, market it, and achieving good results and this happens because of the series of decisions.

*Our World has offered infinite possibilities to take decisions. If you want to learn, start finding ways.*Keep pulling and pushing smartly. Here I pull the money and push myself to do the tasks. First, I saved my money, and second, I learn new activities every day. Knowledge and art are a series of your decisions. The better you accept and implement the better you get success without any dependence on anyone.

Where you can't invest money, invest your mind and every deal will become profitable because your mind is gifted and it's priceless.

CHAPTER THREE

THE REAL WILL FOR DECISION MAKING

What if we climb from the terrace, we would die. Obviously or maybe not. *Everything has a conclusion and it's better if we already know it. Most of people get afraid to take fearless decisions because they get afraid of the results.*But what will happen if we already have the will to accept the results of our decisions? We should develop our will for every situation so that we would have the courage to take better and hard decisions in the future. If you don't get prepared for everything, you would lose easily. Take decisions but ready for the worst. When you accept what you already expected to know, you feel a little worried than to feel hard and harsh on your decisions.

If a stock trader invests money the in stock market then, what can happen to the most, he may be able to lose all his money and that's it. *Money and Relationships are the cause of our daily life worries.*If we remove money from success, most of the problems get solved. Prepare the will and habit to bear any kind of risk. Think about what can happen to the most and you will be able to continue your habits of good decision making. When an author releases a new book, it may sell or not or he would lose his money and time invested but that doesn't mean the author should halt his writing journey. *One bad decision is not the real trademark to stop taking wise decisions. The more you feel afraid, the more mistakes you will do.*So, to take hard decisions you should already know the conclusions already and give time to accept anything. I release books every month and some books get fail miserably but it doesn't mean I should stop writing books. My will is intact to understand the decision making of life.

Take hard decisions, hope for the best but please ready for the worst and you can still take decisions like a pro.

CHAPTER FOUR

FOOL YOUR MIND

The Mind is the brilliant conscious part of the brain that can help us to achieve any heights in life but sometimes it destroys us when we don't understand it well.I'm always telling the hard decisions because we always have to face critical decisions where we get confused. After all, our mind feels all the options correct. We all were confused to take science, art or commerce stream after high school but we all went for what our family tradition follows or maybe we decided to do something unique. Sometimes our mind also fools us because we all have a lot of information hidden in our subconscious mind and that pushes us to take decisions that aren't actually ours but we still think it as ours. Our mind fools us most of the time. Yes, it's not the theory but if you look back you will realise that once you wanted to choose differently but our mind went with the flow.

Now it's our time to make our mind fool. My aim to write this chapter is to understand the power of your mind. **Don't take decisions only for money and emotions.Be late but accurate for your decisions.**Don't let the latent information become dominant in your current decisions. You should know what you are actually doing. Maybe you wanted to become an artist or businessman but because of the flow, you become something else. The reality is different. Maybe you didn't take that decision but the information in your mind pushed you to do that. We see and learn but not everything is real. Social and real lives are much different. People are doing much well even without a social life. We should have art to balance our different roles in people's life. When we connect with many people, we should know how to get our decisions unaffected with their information and that's where you can win and take unbiased decisions of your life.

When it comes to success, every decision is important, and much important is how well you use your own information than to get pushed by someone else.

CHAPTER FIVE

THE FAQ OF DECISION MAKING

Yes, you read it right and this chapter wasn't on my list because who cares for the FAQ of any website or any book. And I think writers don't write such chapters but according to my opinion it's significant and people should read it. Remember the few points before taking any decision in your life:

Q. Why I prefer only hard decisions and not smart decisions? Everyone is talking about smart and you are talking about hard.

A. Because you don't only have to take decisions but to accept it later because the decisions have a great impact on your life. It's about being strong and I believe hard is a much better term for it.

Q. I want to take hard decisions but people don't give me an opportunity.

A. Become the centre attraction of your art and people will surely come and respect your decisions.

Q.I have taken terrible decisions in life. What should I do?

A.As I said no decision is right or wrong but the reality is the acceptance of our mind. Once you accept it you will find opportunities in between them.

Q.I want to become an artist but my parents wanted me to do the job?

A.That's an important question. Respect your parents and if possible follow your art with your daily job duty. Maybe it's hard but once you prove yourself, they would surely love to believe in your art. You have to make believe yourself and your parents. Don't lose hope. Word hard.

Q.People make fun of my decisions.

A.Look we can't convince everyone with our decisions. Your decisions should first right to you and your family. It's not easy to win different minds with a single mind.

When you take hard decisions, you increase the chance of your success. The early you take the better you become in your life.

About The Author

Deepak Gupta is an enthralling Indian author with the great art of gripping storytelling. He is the *#1 Bestselling Author of "She" and The Power of Nothing*. He was born in Delhi, India. He graduated in commerce from Ramjas College, Delhi University and completed his Masters in Commerce from Delhi school of economics. Recently his three books including *10 Principles to Beat Failure, The Lost Child, and Earth 2200* were selected under *Google Best Choice Award 2018*. His ardency for inditing is authentically incontrovertible and unmatchable. He believes in inditing the best exceptional content from his subconscious mind. He loves to observe, absorb and write on various social issues, inspirational truthful words, short stories, and heart whelming poetry. He has travelled to many places in India like Manali, Rajasthan, Goa, Kolkata, Madhya Pradesh, Jammu, Dalhousie, and Mussoorie to bring descent originality in his work. He *releases new short books every month* to get readers to connect with the truth of life. He lives in Delhi with his parents. You can electronically *mail him at guptadeepak3111994@gmail.com* and follow him on *twitter@authordeepakgup* and *Instagram @authordeepakgupta* or like his official Facebook fan page *(https://www.facebook.com/authordeepakgupta/).*

You can visit his official website: **www.authordeepakgupta.com**